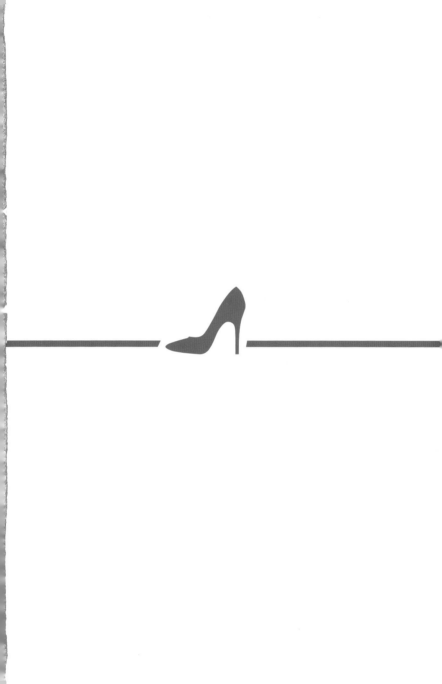

A STUDIO PRESS BOOK

First published in the UK in 2024 by Studio Press,
an imprint of Bonnier Books UK,
4th Floor, Victoria House, Bloomsbury Square,
London WC1B 4DA
Owned by Bonnier Books, Sveavägen 56, Stockholm, Sweden

www.bonnierbooks.co.uk

1 3 5 7 9 10 8 6 4 2

ISBN 978-1-80078-956-2

Written by Jessica Bumpus
Edited by Stephanie Milton
Designed by Maddox Philpot
Picture Research by Paul Ashman
Production by Giulia Caparrelli

This book is unofficial and unauthorised and
is not endorsed by or affiliated with Manolo Blahnik

A CIP catalogue record for this book
is available from the British Library

Printed and bound in China

The publisher would like to thank the following for supplying photos for
this book: Alamy, Getty and Shutterstock. Every effort
has been made to obtain permission to reproduce copyright material but
there may be cases where we have not been able to trace a copyright holder.
The publisher will be happy to correct any omissions in future printing.

# MANOLO BLAHNIK

## The Story Behind the Style

JESSICA BUMPUS

# Contents

LEFT: Manolo Blahnik at Bergdorf Goodman, October 2010, New York City, for *Manolo's New Shoes* book signing.

# A Household Name is Born

There is no name in footwear that can conjure quite the same response as Manolo Blahnik, whose delectable confections (there really is no other way to describe them) have dressed the feet of film stars and fashion's finest for over five decades.

His designs – which are referred to simply as "Manolos" – are synonymous with joy, verve, exuberance and fun; and, of course, with the fictional Carrie Bradshaw from the smash-hit 1990s and 2000s TV show, *Sex and the City*. New York received quite the pavement pounding courtesy of Mr Blahnik's and Ms Bradshaw's predilection for strappy sandals and seriously pointy shoes, and simultaneously ignited a shoe-shopping fetish among women everywhere.

But the story of Manolo Blahnik began a long time before the world was introduced to Sarah Jessica Parker's Carrie Bradshaw. Blahnik is responsible for designing some of the most iconic footwear fashion has ever seen – there are but a handful of footwear designers whose names and designs are so widely known, who have stood the test of time, or who ignite quite such a thrill. Blahnik's creations are quite literally the lofty heights of shoe design – in some cases, his elegant heels reach in excess of 10cm.

OPPOSITE: Manolo Blahnik
poses for a portrait for
*New York* Magazine, 2002.

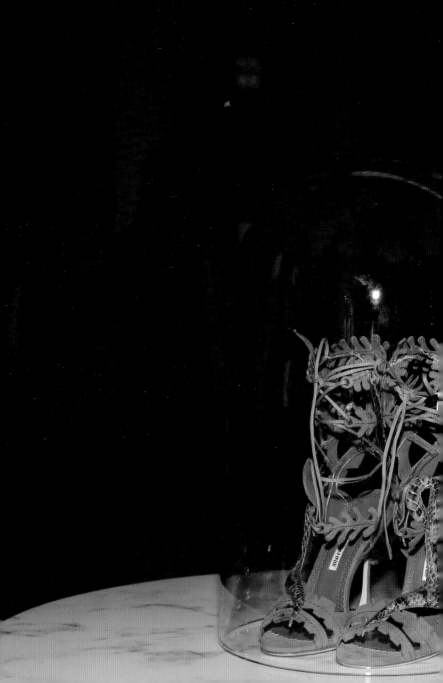

Manolo Blahnik was born on November 27, 1942, in Santa Cruz de la Palma in the Canary Islands, to a Spanish mother and a Czech father. He has claimed that shoes are in his DNA and that both of his parents loved them; he was always surrounded by beautiful footwear. Yet it was not obvious that designing footwear would be his career path – this appears to have been something of an accident, and occurred thanks to the legendary fashion editor Diana Vreeland.

As it happens, it was a very happy accident for all concerned (not to mention feet everywhere), in fashion and film, as well as the general public. Blahnik has been honoured with many awards; and exhibitions have celebrated him over the years. Those he has worked with include fashion designers Ossie Clark, Calvin Klein, Azzedine Alaïa, Oscar de la Renta, Grace Wales Bonner and the superstar singer Rihanna. Celebrities and film stars Hailey Bieber, Zoë Kravitz, Margot Robbie, Reese Witherspoon, Paul Mescal, Penn Badgley, Seth Rogen, Maggie Gyllenhaal, Katie Holmes and more have all worn his designs – often on the red carpet. The editor of American *Vogue*, Anna Wintour, also regularly wears Manolos – no mean feat, indeed. The pair are reported to be friends, and she has been a great champion of his.

By his own admission, Blahnik is a workaholic who loves nothing more than to be at home with his dogs, drawing. His niece, Kristina, who became the company's CEO in 2013, recalls as a child wanting to play with him, while he was sketching.

PREVIOUS: Manolo Blahnik at the premiere of *Manolo: The Boy Who Made Shoes for Lizards*, New York, 2017.

OPPOSITE: Manolo Blahnik at his boutique in New York City, 1982.

If you happen to wander past one of his shops in London – the most famous is the original Old Church Street premises in Chelsea, another is in Burlington Arcade and the latest on Old Burlington Street – the fruits of this obsession, and his success, will twinkle back at you. A Manolo Blahnik window is like the grown-up version of a sweet shop.

Blahnik is known for his imaginative designs, and this should come as no surprise. His idyllic childhood, growing

up amid colourful, lush surroundings teeming with all manner of life, from lizards to exotic plants, has provided plenty of inspiration over the years, though he now also calls England home, some of the time.

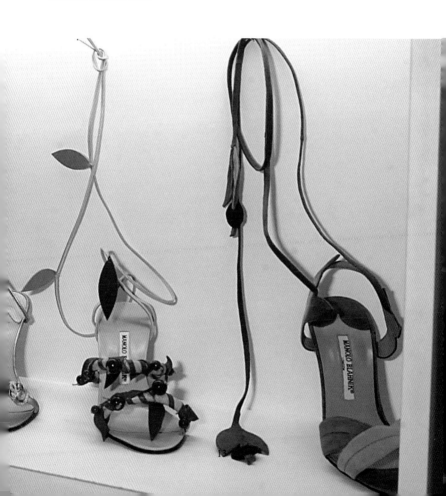

# The Canary Islands

Famously, as a child, Manolo Blahnik would create shoes for the lizards he shared his home with. He grew up on a banana plantation in the Canary Islands, so nature was right there on his doorstep and lizards were a common sight. He soon decided they were to be his models; he would fashion little shoes for them using the aluminium wrappers from sweets – and so the story goes, the lizards also received dresses designed by the young Blahnik. They were not the only recipients – he would fashion little slippers for his dog, although legend has it these weren't quite so successful.

The story was turned into a modern fairytale-meets-memoir by the designer himself, and his friend, Camilla Morton, for *A Fashion Fairy Tale Memoir: Manolo Blahnik and the Tale of the Elves and the Shoemaker*. Well-known for his lyrical and colourful sketches, Blahnik also illustrated the book, which was published in 2011.

The designer and his younger sister, Evangelina, were schooled at home and enjoyed a childhood full of imaginary games and time spent outside. There were few neighbours around and there was no television, which meant no distractions.

He was inspired by both of his parents when it came to fashion – they were both enthusiastic about the subject. Fashion magazines like *Vogue* and *Harper's Bazaar* were sent to the island and his mother would visit the local seamstress; his father also had clothes tailor-made.

Blahnik found himself quite captivated by fashion magazines, especially *Vogue* and the glamorous world it represented. At the time, shoes were not the primary

focus in the fashion world, although they would become a significant priority later on. When Blahnik was growing up, shoes were thought to complete an outfit, whereas today the purchase of a pair of shoes will often be the first step towards building an outfit.

It was thanks to his mother that Blahnik came to recognise the importance of shoes. She had learned to make her own footwear and it is clear that she was a significant inspiration and influence on him. Blahnik's designs were so compelling that he would help change the pecking order of getting dressed – an outfit would be built around his designs, rather than the other way round.

ABOVE: The Canary
Islands, Spain.

Books and films have also been a great source of inspiration for the designer. According to the book *Vogue On: Manolo Blahnik*, at one point his film collection was at 28,000; and he often has 5 to 6 books on the go at once.

As a teen, he loved books about Britain, especially those about the lives of the British upper classes. Authors of interest include Evelyn Waugh, Nancy Mitford and Cecil

Beaton. His style, both personal and in terms of design, has always belonged to another era, and this has been of great benefit when it comes to his shoes. For example, he was not a fan of the 1970s-style clompy platform, and instead offered stilettos as an elegant and chic alternative. He has always been described as something of a snappy dresser, and is instantly recognisable due to his trademark big smile and glasses.

Blahnik was educated at home until the age of 11, then went on to a boarding school in Villiers in Switzerland – his parents had decided he needed to experience more than just island life, lovely though it was. He would go on to study International Law at the University of Geneva but it didn't suit him and he was rather uninspired, so switched to a literature degree. He graduated in 1965. His next stop was a city he had often visited while staying in Geneva.

ABOVE: The University of Geneva where Blahnik studied International Law, followed by Literature.

# Paris

Blahnik left Geneva and headed to Paris in 1965, where he studied art and theatre design at the École des Beaux Arts and the École du Louvre respectively. He worked first in an antique shop and then later at a store named Go, on the Left Bank, where he carved out a reputation for himself through his charisma and his aesthetic. It was here he met Paloma Picasso, the daughter of the famous artist Pablo. Paloma would go on to have quite the impact on his career, but there would also be others.

On a trip to New York at the turn of the 1970s, Paloma introduced Blahnik to the legendary fashion editor Diana Vreeland, who had famously worked at *Harper's Bazaar* US before snagging the editor-in-chief position at American *Vogue*. Her bold personality – demonstrated through her style and her quotable fashion mantras, of which there are many – ensured she became a leading figure in the fashion industry.

At this point in time, it's thought that she had just been ousted from American *Vogue*. She would go on to be a consultant to the Costume Institute at the Metropolitan Museum of Art.

Blahnik presented Vreeland with his portfolio which featured drawings of sets and costumes, but it was the shoes that caught her eye. It was in that instant that she told Blahnik what he should focus his talents on: shoes.

The pair became friends, and he credits Vreeland for his eureka moment – a moment that changed the course of his life, not to mention the footwear choices of women everywhere, for the rest of time. Blahnik returned to London with a plan.

PREVIOUS LEFT: The Eiffel Tower, Paris, circa 1960s.

PREVIOUS RIGHT: École Nationale des Beaux Arts.

LEFT: The woman who told Manolo to create shoes: Diana Vreeland.

# Important Friendships

Paloma Picasso and Diana Vreeland would not be the only women of influence in Manolo's life. His mother had already played a significant role, as had another family member – his father's cousin. Aunt Frederique was married to the Greek Ambassador to Switzerland; she was stylish and had an eye for detail – traits which appealed to Blahnik.

As a teenager, he had a hunger for culture and love for elegance, and subsequently developed a great interest in international figures who epitomised this, such as the Empress of Austria.

Blahnik would also find these traits in the fashion collector and jewellery designer Tina Chow, the actress Anjelica Huston, the late Italian fashion magpie Anna Piaggi, model Bianca Jagger, American *Vogue*'s Grace Coddington and Anna Wintour, and the late fashion icon Isabella Blow.

RIGHT: Paloma Picasso,
Manolo Blahnik's friend.

Anna Wintour was actually one of Blahnik's first customers when she was living in London in the 1980s, and it is from this that their friendship grew. She is often photographed wearing a certain style: custom versions of the Callasli, which Blahnik simply refers to now as the "AW".

OPPOSITE: Fashion icon
and writer, Anna Piaggi.

ABOVE: Jack Nicholson and Anjelica
Huston at the Academy Awards, 1974.

# London

B lahnik moved to London in 1969 amid a landmark cultural moment. It was the Swinging Sixties, a time of Youthquake revolution, and Blahnik was hanging out with equally exciting new names in the creative field. He found that he was quickly able to charm the fashion world which he had admired for so long, and of which he would so soon be a permanent fixture.

Blahnik visited London frequently while living and studying in Paris. For him, the city held a certain kind of creative fascination, both socially and artistically, and he would make friends there which would increase his fondness.

But he needed a work permit to be able to stay. He got a job at Feathers, a popular boutique in Kensington, where he learned a great deal about both fashion and retail. He also caught the eye of various members of the fashion press (including *Vogue*'s Caterine Millinaire), who often frequented the store, which was known as one of London's most fashionable boutiques.

While working here, he made friends with artist and photographer Eric Boman, and befriended a set decorator called Peter Young who would also play a key role in Blahnik's creative career. There was a small shop on Old Church Street in Chelsea, called Zapata, and Blahnik and Young decorated the interior of the petite shoe shop.

Blahnik enjoyed it and was keen to take on more work in this vein. Ultimately, set decoration would not satisfy this future designer's creative pulse; he was looking for something more.

By the early 1970s, he had taken that all-important trip to New York with Paloma; by the time he returned, the wheels were already in motion and soon after, Blahnik became a design consultant at Zapata. He designed his first pair of shoes for men. Friends, including the painter David Hockney, wore them but they were not successful commercially. No matter – Blahnik's big break was just around the corner.

ABOVE: The artist David Hockney, circa 1978, wore the early designs of Manolo Blahnik.

# Ossie Clark

With great success comes a learning curve or two. One of the most charming tales of this nature involves Manolo Blahnik designing shoes for the legendary Ossie Clark.

Clark was well-known for his expert cutting and ethereal, vintage-looking designs – featuring the bold and captivating prints of his wife, Celia Birtwell – which made their mark from the mid-1960s to the mid-1970s. To this day, Clark's designs are revered for their grace and technicality.

Teaming up with Clark would turn out to be Blahnik's big break. A mutual friend had introduced him to London's big star and, hitting it off immediately, Clark commissioned Blahnik to make the shoes for his spring/summer 1972 collection which took place in 1971.

The only problem was Blahnik's lack of technical know-how – he had never formally trained to make shoes, he had just learned what he could along the way. In the case of this particular commission, he had forgotten to put heels in that would support the shoe – the rubber heels didn't have steel inside, which caused the shoes to wobble and the models had to make a concerted effort to stay upright.

---

OPPOSITE: Ossie Clark, 1967.

The joke was that Blahnik had invented a new way to walk, but in interviews years later the designer often shared this all-too-relatable tale of failure which came at such a crucial time.

Nevertheless, the shoes were beautiful and typically Manolo Blahnik. Reportedly, ten designs featured, including a design with red cherries wrapped around the ankle, and a green sandal with a rubber heel. Luckily, no one else seemed to notice the mishap – and if they did they clearly forgave the designer. In 2021, the brand celebrated its 50th anniversary.

RIGHT: Circa 1970. A design by Ossie Clark, with whom Manolo would collaborate.

# The 1970s

This was an important decade for Manolo Blahnik. His career was taking off, he was working with designers and he was being featured in magazines. Despite initially thinking his career was about to end because of the Ossie Clark wobble, in reality the opposite was true.

LEFT: Manolo Blahnik, 1979.

In 1973, with a loan of £2,000, Blahnik bought out the owner of Zapata and opened his own boutique on Old Church Street. The shop became so successful in just three years, that he was able to pay back the loan in full. He enlisted his sister Evangelina, with whom he had always been close, to help build the business. Blahnik noted that he wasn't interested in opening a hundred branches or teaming up with big businesses. Today, according to the Manolo Blahnik website, there are more than 300 points of sale, including 20 flagships, and the brand has collaborated with a handful of big names on special projects.

Blahnik's Old Church Street outpost would become a destination spot, with movie stars including Lauren Bacall dropping in to the shop, as well as Jane Birkin and Charlotte Rampling. The fashion editors of the time were also known to frequent the store – including Grace Coddington, who helped put Blahnik in *Vogue*.

For Kansai Yamamoto, he designed The Brick shoe, which featured in the Japanese designer's first collection in 1971; in 1977, Bianca Jagger wore her Manolo Blahniks while making that memorable entrance at Studio 54; and the Knot design, featuring a knot at its front, debuted in 1978. His shoes were becoming the hot ticket, offering something new, elegant and against the grain of the fashions of the time. Stilettos also made a comeback under his watchful eye.

---

OPPOSITE: At an Ossie Clark fashion show, 1970. Blahnik's collaboration with the designer would help launch his career.

# *Vogue*

B lahnik first encountered the American issue of *Vogue* when he was young – it was one of the magazines his mother would receive in the Canary Islands and he, too, would eagerly await its arrival. Little did he know that years later, he and his designs would feature in it regularly. Coincidentally, one of *Vogue*'s legendary editors would play a part in selecting his career direction.

During his early days working in London, Blahnik befriended many of *Vogue*'s young editors. His shoes were featured sometimes under the name Zapata, or Manolo Blahnik for Zapata, from about 1972 onwards. To this day, if you flip through an issue of *Vogue*, you will likely find Blahnik's name credited among the glossy pages.

Blahnik became the second man ever to appear on the front cover of *Vogue*, for the January 1974 British issue. He was photographed by David Bailey and styled by Grace Coddington, posing with Anjelica Huston. With glasses in hand, and the sea stretching out behind them, the coverline chimes "Happy New Year". Inside was a 14-page fashion story photographed in the South of France and Corsica. Blahnik notes that he had a lot of fun on that shoot.

ABOVE: Manolo Blahnik's niece, Kristina Blahnik, photographed for *Vogue* Magazine, 2010, London, England.

# MANOLO BLAHNIK

# The Anatomy of a Manolo Blahnik Design

When Manolo Blahnik began designing shoes, he wasn't interested in following trends – and to this day, this is still the case. At the start of his career he found the prevailing popularity for platforms not to fit with his taste. Over the years Blahnik's designs have been recognised for their slim and elegant arched heels, their pointed toes, a hint of toe cleavage, jewel-hued tones as well as regal decoration, and fastening ties that climb around the ankle like an exotic plant. Not to mention the classics, such as the sandal design favoured by Anna Wintour.

Blahnik has several trademarks, but it's his use of ornamentation that has really set him apart from his contemporaries. He is an expert in utilising tassels, fringe and more to create fantasy footwear. Notably, the buckle is also his hardware of choice and he is known for creating embellished versions which look like they could have stepped out of the pages of history books.

Best known of these buckled beauties is probably the Hangisi shoe – the very shoe that Mr Big (Chris Noth) uses to propose to Carrie Bradshaw in the *Sex and the City* film (he does so with a blue version). The design is said to feature 21 components, including nails, heel tip, lining, foam and padding, and has become quite the shoe icon.

PREVIOUS:
Inside "Manolo
Blahnik: The
Art of Shoes"
at Nacional
de las Artes
Decorativas
Museum,
Madrid, Spain,
2017.

RIGHT: The
Hangisi
design at Saks
Fifth Avenue,
New York City.

# The Hangisi

Blahnik told *Footwear News* that he had dreamed up the style after a trip to Palermo, Italy, where he saw an exhibition by Giovanni Boldini, an Italian portraitist, who painted society ladies in the late 19th and early 20th centuries. The buckles on their shoes had caught his eye.

Since then, the Hangisi has been produced in over 100 materials and colours, across boots, flats and mules. On the Hangisi's 10th anniversary in 2018, Blahnik joked that it was a never-ending line. He also mentioned that, upon its creation, he had no idea just how popular it would be – he never anticipated that it would be such an icon among his work, and within the footwear industry generally.

ABOVE: Flat versions of the Hangisi, recognisable for its jewel colours and ornate buckle, inspired by Napoleon I, Josephine and Pauline Bonaparte.

BELOW: Blahnik's jewellery for the feet at Saks Fifth Avenue.

# Jewellery for the Feet

Manolo Blahnik's use of buckles brings a sense of history to the designs, which feel majestic and grand. As a result, his shoes have often been compared to jewellery for the feet – the Okkato pump also shines with ornate hardware.

Chains, feathers, ribbons, rings and silk brocade are also part of his stylistic repertoire – tactile touches that stand out in an era of mass production. Blahnik is known for handcrafting each shoe prototype himself.

His use of construction and attention to detail also make him stand out – innovative heels with shapely holes in the

ABOVE LEFT: A Blahnik boot featuring rich embroidery at the Museum of Decorative Arts in Madrid, 2017.

ABOVE RIGHT: Blahnik's pompom design on show at the Museum of Decorative Arts in Madrid, 2017.

middle, such as 2022's "Eye Heel", inspired by Elizabeth Taylor's eyeliner to create an internal almond silhouette; or spring/summer 2012's Bohu sandal referencing Henri Matisse with figures dancing around the ankle strap; or 2001's Lyonnia sandals ornate in pink garden roses which were a favourite flower of his friend Cecil Beaton. His toe shapes are also striking. Yet, interestingly, they never look out of place, clunky or avant-garde.

According to the brand, the shoes are offered in a wide range of sizes, typically 35.5 to 41.5, with heels and lasts scaled proportionally. In shoemaking, a last is a wooden carved representation of the foot on which the shoe is made. Heel heights are available from 10mm to 115mm across various designs.

To celebrate 50 years of Manolo Blahnik, the brand released

ABOVE: A design which shows the historial influence of Blahnik's creations.

OPPOSITE: A bejwelled design in front of its sketch.

a gold capsule collection which revisited recognisable trimmings and styles for a shimmering update. It included a theatrical knee-high boot, the Flequillohi, with tiered fringing and trimmed with a ribbon of black beading, as well as the Maysale mule, featuring renewed embellishments such as gold-tone hardware with glowing citrine crystals. The collection sold out – a gilded success.

# Collaborations, Part 1

Today, collaborations are a common and well-documented part of the fashion industry. In fact, they have always occurred – and for Blahnik they helped him to learn his craft as well as establish, and further, his network.

In the early days, Blahnik collaborated with British fashion designer Jean Muir, known for simple but flattering silhouettes, as well as Fiorucci, founded by Elio Fiorucci in 1967. The latter took him to Italy's factories, where he

refined his talent. It was a meeting of minds in terms of colour and fanciful designs and, for Blahnik, it contributed some financial stability.

When Muir was selected as Designer of the Year at Bath Fashion Museum in 1979, the black jersey dress and leather jacket were paired with a pair of Blahnik's heels. His shoes would also be paired with another winner, Sheridan Barnett, in 1983.

OPPOSITE:
Elio Fiorucci and Manolo Blahnik, Milan, 2012.

RIGHT: A Jean Muir magazine advert, circa 1970s.

Jean Muir
at Selfridges
Soft, sensuous matte jersey dress.
Almond, fudge, black or red. Sizes
8 to 16. £108. Hat to order, £16.
**Selfridges** Design Room

# Going to America

In 1979, Manolo Blahnik opened his first store on Madison Avenue, New York – having been stocked at Bloomingdale's the year before, following the launch of his first US collection. The American business would take off in the 1980s. He would open a store on West 54th Street in 1983.

It's worth noting that at the time, Blahnik's exuberant designs were rather bodacious given the typically conservative US dress sense, but nevertheless, distribution agreements were made with Barneys, Bergdorf Goodman and Neiman Marcus.

George Malkemus, a copywriter in Bergdorf Goodman's marketing department, was tasked with running the American wing of the company – an appointment which had come through Dawn Mello, an executive vice-president of Bergdorf Goodman.

Blahnik would go on to design shoes for various other big American names of the day. Calvin Klein approached him to create shoes for his ready-to-wear collection; Blahnik also worked with Anne Klein and became good friends with Isaac Mizrahi, for whom he would design the Maysale pump for the spring/summer 1991 collection.

By the end of the 1980s, one of Blahnik's early champions, Anna Wintour, had landed in NYC. She was now the editor of *House & Garden* magazine, which likely helped his profile grow. But he had already been doing pretty well: *USA Today* predicted that the New York store would do a million dollars' worth of trade by the end of 1984 and Blahnik was being recognised by the Council of Fashion Designers of America for an award. America would continue to play a huge role in the evolution of the brand during the 1990s.

In 2021, an expansive flagship opened at 717 Madison Avenue. Inspired by the glamour of Hollywood Regency, it was designed by the interior decorator David Thomas with a symmetrical layout, so that men's shoes were on one side and women's on the other.

OPPOSITE TOP: The iconic streets of New York City.

# The 1980s

Blahnik credits Perry Ellis, the American sportswear designer, for properly introducing him to America. In the 1980s, it was apparently Ellis's assistant, Patricia Pastor, who fell for the magic of Blahnik's shoes when she saw them in his new store.

At the time, Ellis was considered quite the darling of the American fashion scene, and Blahnik made all his shoes. Other American brands Blahnik worked with during his career included Calvin Klein, Bill Blass, Oscar de la Renta, Carolina Herrera, Geoffrey Beene and Isaac Mizrahi.

For Blahnik's first collaboration with Mizrahi in 1988 he created the Rodriga desert boot. In a break from fashion runway trends at the time, the designer showed this boot with every single one of his looks.

As Blahnik's knowledge of craftsmanship and shoe making grew, his designs became more impressive. By the mid-1980s, his shoes were said to be noticeably bolder and more extravagant, more in line with the styles we associate with him today.

OPPOSITE: Perry Ellis and Manolo Blahnik at Mr Chow's restaurant in New York City, 1980, with Andy Warhol in the background.

# Craftsmanship

Craft lies at the heart of the Manolo Blahnik brand, though Blahnik will point out that it wasn't until the mid-1980s that he really began to get to grips with this. The turning point was a trip to Italy, to the factories just outside Milan. He was keen to learn everything – he watched how the shoes were made, studying the work process and every small detail, until he, too, knew how to make perfect shoes.

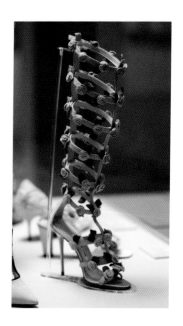

Blahnik loves being in Milan and working with his team as he oversees the practical shoe-making process. He will spend weeks at a time visiting his factories in Italy.

For Blahnik, the heel is the most important part of the design – a lesson he learned early on from the shoes he designed for Ossie Clark. He will personally carve each heel himself until it is right. Today, whether clients like high or modest heels or flats, there is something to suit everyone.

The accessories and techniques he uses include: buckles, feathers, fringing, pompoms, metalwork, tassels, studs and eyelets, patchwork, pleating, laser-cut, embroidery, beading, applique, top-stitching, knotting and latticework.

While the shoes themselves are beautiful and compelling, inviting you to slip a foot in, Cinderalla-style, comfort is also important. His consideration of comfort is another reason Blahnik has been so successful – it is said to be something even cobblers have commented on.

# King of Colour

Sketching and painting are important parts of Blahnik's design process. As a young boy, he would paint, using watercolours, with his mother. He recently revealed to *The Blend* magazine that in the 1980s, he began using Dr. Ph. Martin's ink. This kind of ink, he says, is the best –he likes it for its lightness and texture.

Colour is tremendously important to Blahnik and he approaches it in a bold way. To see a wall of his sketches – whimsical visions inspired by other worlds – or a shop floor or window full of his shoes, is testament to that.

Colour is arguably one of Blahnik's unique selling points; he conjurs rich, bright hues from moments in history, nature, books, films and geographical locations, then lets his creative mind do the rest.

Insider tip: according to *The Blend*, Blahnik buys all his inks and sketching materials from Green & Stone of Chelsea.

OPPOSITE: A presentation at London Fashion Week, spring/summer 2014.

RIGHT: A Manolo Blahnik design alongside its sketch.

OVERLEAF: Manolo Blahnik with his designs on show at Museum of Decorative Arts in Madrid.

# Fans

A great many people have worn Manolo Blahniks, and with every awards season or television appearance that number contiues to grow. This includes fashion insiders, such as Bianca Jagger and Isabella Blow, as well as the late Diana, Princess of Wales – and more recently the Maestro actress Carey Mulligan who wore Carolyne, a slingback pump, on *The Tonight Show Starring Jimmy Fallon*.

Diana, Princess of Wales wore Manolos until her death in 1997. Famously, she wore a pair of Blahnik's shoes to the Serpentine Gallery party in 1994 with Christina Stambolian's off-the-shoulder black dress, now more commonly referred to as "The Revenge Dress".

Kate Middleton, now Princess of Wales and the daughter-in-law of the late Diana, wears Manolo Blahnik, too – including the famous Hangisi design.

Meanwhile, Isabella Blow, the late fashion editor of *Tatler* and a great supporter of Blahnik's, wore a pointed pair of witchy shoes for her wedding to Detmar Blow in Gloucester Cathedral in 1989. It is easy to see how his theatrical styles would appeal to her.

There is even a rumour that Marge Simpson's classic red shoes are Manolo Blahnik... wouldn't that be rather fun?

Victoria Beckham, who is almost always spotted in a pair of heels, wears Manolo Blahnik and also worked with the designer on her spring/summer 2013 show – interestingly enough, on this occasion the shoes featured in the show were flats and not heels!

Meghan Markle is also known to be a fan of the classic BB styles.

---

RIGHT: The late Diana, Princess of Wales in "The Revenge Dress", coordinated with a pair of Manolos.

# The 1990s

M anolo Blahnik remembers that he worked a lot during the 1990s. It was arguably the decade in which the brand became a household name. It wasn't just down to *Sex and the City* (where we started to become familiar with pointed and strappy numbers), it was also due to the creation of collections for some of America's biggest fashion names, including his friend Isaac Mizrahi, and spending time partaking in special appearances and touring the country.

In 1994, Blahnik created runway collections for Bill Blass, Carolina Herrera and Oscar de la Renta. His designs would subsequently go on to accompany those of international designers such as Michael Kors, Todd Oldham, Clements Ribeiro, Antonio Berardi, Matthew Williamson and John Galliano.

Cynthia Marcus, of the famed department store Neiman Marcus, declared that Blahnik was so important that if he had wanted to change the name of the store to Neiman Blahnik, she would have done it.

Apparently for two years from 1990, there wasn't a single issue of *Vogue* without a pair of Manolo Blahnik's in them.

OPPOSITE: Isaac Mizrahi with Manolo Blahnik shoes for autumn/winter 1990.

# John Galliano, Dior

Gibraltar-born John Galliano was a leading light in the British fashion industry when he graduated from Central Saint Martins in 1984. At the time, his bright star shone alongside fellow upcomer Alexander McQueen. Galliano's designs, a collection titled "Les Incroyables" which had been inspired by the French Revolution, were snapped up by

Browns, the well-known fashion boutique on South Molton Street.

He was appointed head designer of the House of Dior in 1996, but would work with Blahnik on shoes for his own collections and that of the historic Paris house. For Galliano's own collections, he used Blahnik's "Agatha" design, a reference apparently to Miss Marple, and it has continued to be associated with their collaboration. It first appeared around 1994 to 1995.

The designer also created the "Galli" for Galliano's autumn/winter 1995 collection, which Blahnik's website described as featuring metalwork.

On another occasion, Blahnik refers to a "fantasy" design for Galliano: his take on the historical chopine, a style of flatform clog worn by Venetian women from the 15th century to the early 17th, though it's unclear if this was real or hypothetical as it was never put into production.

Galliano said that Blahnik was an innovator and has a great understanding of women's feet and legs.

Today, Galliano is still considered a leading name in fashion, heading up the house of Margiela on couture.

OPPOSITE: Rosita Missoni, Manolo Blahnik and John Galliano, 2016.

# Influences
# and Inspirations

B lahnik is well-travelled (though he has confessed he hates airports), and this is reflected in his work. He creates more than just a shoe: he creates a woman and a world – arguably, his designs are akin to objets d'art that could be displayed like treasures.

Blahnik has been influenced by a number of countries including Spain, Italy, Greece and Russia; his work is a reflection of theatre, history, botany, nature, and many more things besides. Each of his designs starts from a sketch – a whimsical affair often annotated to equally dreamy effect.

LEFT: Manolo Blahnik sketching in the documentray *Manolo: The Boy Who Made Shoes for Lizards,* 2017.

When people talk about Manolo Blahnik, they will often mention his encyclopaedic knowledge of the arts, films and books. In 2011, to celebrate the 15th anniversary of the British *Vogue* website, he selected his 15 favourite black-and-white films to mark the occasion; on his website, he also shares gardening tips and film recommendations.

LEFT: A Manolo Blahnik advert from the 1990s.

MANOLO BLAHNIK®

During 2020's lockdown, he shared his inspirations with Forbes: listening to Janis Joplin and reading Giuseppe Tomasi di Lampedusa's *The Leopard*, which has been a favourite of his ever since he was a child. He equally adores the film version by Luchino Visconti. He said that he was keeping himself amused by sketching, which he did most days, reading and watching films, and that men's shoes were a particular focus for him.

It's all of these interests, pastimes and hobbies that have provided Blahnik with such glorious inspiration and which make his designs so unique.

OPPOSITE: Manolo Blahnik, 2017, from *The Boy Who Made Shoes for Lizards*.

RIGHT: More pompoms in this Manolo Blahnik design.

BELOW: An ornate heel to match its ornate sketch.

# *Sex and the City*

On June 6, 1998, a new television show called *Sex and the City* aired on HBO. Blahnik had no idea how much of an impact this would have on his career, the future of the Manolo Blahnik brand, and fashion in general.

The show was based on the stories of Candace Bushnell, an American author and journalist, and starred Sarah Jessica Parker as Carrie Bradshaw, a singleton writer/columnist living in Manhattan, along with her three friends. All of them had a penchant for fashion, especially shoes, but none more so than Carrie.

*Sex and the City* brought Manolo Blahnik to the masses – so much so that his shoes simply became known as "Manolos". Carrie could be seen carrying the glossy carrier bags bearing his name almost as frequently as she would sport a designer handbag (usually a Dior saddle bag or a Fendi baguette). Manolos would become the most mentioned fashion brand in the series, which for a fashion-filled television show is an impressive feat.

With a walk-in wardrobe of dreams which had the TARDIS-like ability to house hundreds of shoes, Carrie, of course, had her favourites. There are standout episodes that put Manolos front and centre of the storyline, and had us all wondering how we, too, could lead Carrie's life and wear all of her shoes.

ABOVE: Manolo Blahnik and Sarah Jessica Parker at an event in New York during the early 2000s.

OVERLEAF: Sarah Jessica Parker at Fashion's Night Out 2011 at Manolo Blahnik.

## "Attack of the Five Foot Ten Woman"

In season 3, episode 3, Carrie describes having a religious experience at Manolo Blahnik, where she has just purchased a super-high pair of colourful mules in order to outdo Natasha, Mr Big's new wife.

## "What Goes Around Comes Around"

In season 3, episode 17, Bradshaw takes a wrong turn as she walks the streets of Manhattan. Asking for directions, she finds herself confronted with a mugger who demands her bag, watch, ring and, most upsetting for her, her Manolos – which she got half price at a sample sale.

## "The Good Fight"

In season 4, episode 13, Bradshaw is in a relationship with Aidan Shaw. Things get dicey when his dog, Pete, chews up a pair of turquoise strappy sandals from 1996.

## "A Vogue Idea"

In season 4, episode 17, Bradshaw is freelancing for American *Vogue* when she happens upon the magazine's fashion cupboard. Inside, she is delighted to find the Manolo Blahnik "urban shoe myth": the Mary Jane, rebranded today as the Campari style. Bradshaw tries to squeeze her feet into the pair, despite them not being her size, such is her excitement.

OPPOSITE: Sarah Jessica Parker filming *Sex and the City*, 1998.

BELOW: Sarah Jessica Parker signed her Manolo Blahnik shoes for an auction.

OPPOSITE: The cast of *Sex and the City*, Sarah Jessica Parker, Cynthia Nixon, Kim Cattrall and Kristin Davis, which helped to make Manolo Blahnik famous.

## "A Woman's Right to Shoes"

In season 6, episode 9, Bradshaw attends an old friend's party and, upon arrival, is asked to take her shoes off. The shoes in question are of course Manolo Blahniks, this time in silver – the Sedaraby D'Orsay sandal which, as she points out, are very much part of an outfit. But despite her protestations she is made to take them off.

When it's time to leave, she discovers her shoes are gone – someone has swiped them. She is forced to borrow a pair of sneakers to get home, then have an awkward conversation with her friend, who is reluctant to reimburse Carrie for the cost of such frivolous shoes. In the end, Bradshaw leaves a message to say she is getting married – to herself – and that she is registered at Manolo Blahnik, where the shoes are waiting to be gifted.

## "The Agony and the Ex-tacy"

In season 4, episode 1, Bradshaw is despairing at the fact she is turning 35 and decides to spend the day with her soulmate – Manolo Blahnik. Enough said.

OPPOSITE: Actor Mario Cantone, who plays Anthony in *Sex and the City*, with a Manolo at the *Sex and the City: The Movie – Extended Cut* DVD launch party in 2008.

# The 2000s

It has been said that while *Vogue* brought Manolo Blahnik to fashion consciousness, *Sex and the City* had brought him – the man, as well as the brand – to popular consciousness. Blahnik has acknowledged this and noted his thanks to Sarah Jessica Parker on numerous occasions. He has also pointed out that this surprise cultural moment made his life much easier when it came to breaking America.

The finale episode of the show is estimated to have been watched by 10.6 million people in the US. And the rest of the world was also glued to the screen to wave goodbye to Carrie who had finally achieved her Big happy ending, Manolo Blahnik carrier bag in tow. She is actually carrying one when she speaks to Mr Big on the phone.

Following the smash-hit series came a film in 2008. In it, Mr Big proposes to Carrie (for the second time) with a pair of Manolo Blahniks, which she has gone to retrieve from her soon-to-be-old apartment's closet. In another memorable moment, Mr Big slips the cobalt blue Hangisi shoe onto

OPPOSITE: Manolo Blahnik, circa 2000.

her foot in lieu of a ring (though its embellished buckle does a very good job at standing in). But the brand's success was not confined to *Sex and the City*. Indeed, it was only just beginning. The 2000s also saw further celebration of Manolo Blahnik's work through exhibitions, accolades and awards – and some other surprise artistic outlets.

In 2004, Blahnik designed a shoe horn for the furniture store Habitat as part of its VIP collection. The flashy object was made from silver-plated polished aluminium and came in a curvaceous shape with the designer's name on the outside, and accompanying box. It was among several pieces that saw famous design names put their stamp on household/interior items.

While no longer available to buy in stores, there seems to be a strong resale market for the shoe horn, with various sellers offering what is actually a very useful (if somewhat forgotten) object.

OPPOSITE: Manolo
Blahnik's Habitat
shoe horn.

# Jay-Z's "Bonnie & Clyde"

*Sex and the City* put Manolo Blahnik on television and in the minds of women everywhere. But it wasn't the only piece of popular culture to namecheck the footwear maestro. Along with Burberry and Hermes, in 2002, the Manolo Blahnik name is uttered among the lyrics for Jay-Z's "Bonnie & Clyde" song, which also features Beyoncé on vocals.

Beyoncé and Jennifer Lopez were both clocked wearing the Oklamod booties in music videos which further fueled interest in the designer. At the time, *Sex and the City* was still showing on television and it was clear that Manolo Blahnik was permeating more than just Carrie Bradshaw & Co's wardrobes.

There is also RuPaul, the American drag artist, whose "Click Clack" song released in 2011 mentions Manolo Blahniks – specifically that theirs are going to party that night.

OPPOSITE: Jay-Z and Beyoncé turning heads at The Met Gala in 2015.

OVERLEAF: Manolo Blahnik exhibition at the Wallace Collection, London.

# Design Museum Exhibition

I n 2003, Manolo Blahnik's 30-year career became the subject of a celebratory exhibition at the London Design Museum. Alongside the shoes, visitors could see sketches and rare prototypes, as well as memorabilia from the designer's own archive, and take a look at his photographic and film influences.

Later in 2019, his work also became the subject of an exhibition at the Wallace Collection, *Enquiring Mind*, running from June to October that year. It featured a selection of shoes from his private archive presented to the backdrop of the 18th century rooms and grand artworks, which made for a very Manolo experience. The designer has long had a fascination with the museum – he said it was one of his favourite museums and that he was humbled to have his work on display among its own.

Blahnik co-curated the exhibition along with Dr. Xavier Bray. The idea was to position his designs in the context of the paintings, sculptures and furniture of the museum that had so often inspired him and provoked his enquiring mind.

Across 10 rooms, 160 pairs of shoes were displayed – including, appropriately, those for Sofia Coppola's *Marie Antoinette* film. Displayed in bell jars, their colours and fabrications are as ornate as some of the treasures of the museum, and fit right in.

# Marie Antoinette

Given that Manolo Blahnik has such a love for history and film, it isn't surprising that his reach extends beyond collaborations with fellow designers and into the world of cinema.

In 2006, he worked with the costume designer Milena Canonero on the Sofia Coppola-directed film *Marie Antoinette*. Starring Kirsten Dunst as the let-them-eat-cake queen, it later won an Academy Award for Best Costume Design.

When it came to the shoes, Blahnik told *Footwear News* that he used 18th-century buckles he found in Bath. Apparently, Coppola told him he could do what he wanted. The result was silk taffeta slippers in lovely soft pastels that were almost good enough to eat – Laduree macarons have been used as a comparison by some fashion journalists (side note: in a similar vein, Greta Garbo is thought to have described his shoes as scrumptious). He later said he had loved the experience of working with Coppola and Canonero.

In a book of his drawings titled *Manolo's New Shoes*, Canonero shared that she'd been a fan of his forever – in part because of how he creates characters with his shoes, a sentiment echoed by many of his clients. She also praised his ability to create something beautiful but also comfortable, which she felt was important for actresses in the moment.

Apparently, it was she who suggested to Coppola that they ask Blahnik to make the shoes for the film.

Two particular moments featuring Blahnik's shoes spring to mind when recalling the film: the first is when Dunst as Marie Antoinette is eating cake while a shoe is being placed on her foot by a maid – a shoe as delicious looking as the cake, with ruffles like piped icing or whipped cream. The second is the use of Manolos as props to illustrate Marie Antoinette's emerging fashionability.

ABOVE: At Manolo Blahnik's *The Art of Shoes* exhibition; he designed shoes for the film *Marie Antoinette*, 2006.

OVERLEAF: Manolo Blahnik's shoes take centre stage in the *Marie Antoinette* film.

# Kate Moss

According to the man himself, Kate Moss is one of Blahnik's favourite muses. The British supermodel, like many others, is known to regularly wear his designs – and when she got married to Jamie Hince in 2011, she did so in Manolo Blahnik shoes.

The wedding dress had been custom-made by their mutual friend John Galliano and Blahnik had customised a pair of his multi-strap Godichefac heels for the much-photographed occasion. The design of the shoe is open-toed and fastens with a clasp at the front. It boasts a three-inch heel and is recognisable for its Art Deco aesthetic. At the time, various outlets had reported the sandals as being designed by Christian Louboutin!

But there was a small issue: unable to try them on with the dress until the day before the wedding, Kate discovered that the jewels kept catching on the train, so they were sent to Milan to be fixed. Incredibly, by 8am they were back in the UK and on their way to Moss's wedding. Apparently it had taken five attempts to get them right. The story – or minor fashion fiasco – made headlines in many a daily paper.

OPPOSITE: Kate Moss and Manolo Blahnik, 2003.

of London-based designers to have emerged in recent years,
cusp of design, sculpture and craft.

studied product design at the Vienna Academy of Applied
to enrol at the Royal College of Art. Since graduating in
industrial materials with craft techniques to create exquisite

dous candles on such fine steel wire th
designed two chandeliers fo
re crystals and Stella H

h swathe

# Illustrations

Drawing is something that Blahnik has loved to do ever since he was a child. He has a distinct style – he favours fluid lines and magical charm, somehow managing to perfectly capture the magic of the end product.

Blahnik's drawings have often featured as part of his campaigns. Sometimes his distinctive handwriting annotates his drawings; other times his graphic logo is laid over a sketch.

The designer told *Net-a-Porter* in 2020 that he keeps a sketch pad and a Faber-Castell 3B pencil on a string by his bedside so that if he wakes, he can record an idea.

While fashion illustration is not commonly featured in fashion magazines anymore, Manolo Blahnik's lavish drawings put forward a very good argument for bringing it back as a trend.

PREVIOUS: Jamie Hince and Kate Moss after their wedding, 2011.

OPPOSITE: A Manolo Blahnik magazine advert from the early 2000s.

# MANOLO BLAHNIK

# *The Elves and the Shoemaker*

In 2011, Blahnik and
his fashion writer
friend Camilla Morton
collaborated on a fairy-
tale memoir of his life.
Combining a twist on the
story of "The Elves and
the Shoemaker" with his
own biography, the book
was illustrated by Blahnik
himself. The magical
whimsy of his hand was
ideally suited to bring
such a project to life – the
lizards and dogs of his
childhood were once again
alive and well.

PREVIOUS: Manolo Blahnik
sketches on display at the
Wallace Collection, London.

RIGHT: Manolo Blahnik
and fashion writer
Camilla Morton.

# Praise for Manolo

ABOVE: Manolo Blahnik with Kate Moss and Naomi Campbell at the Council of Fashion Designers of America Awards.

There has never been a shortage of praise for Blahnik. He is widely considered to be a charming character with a great sense of fun, full of stories and passion for his work.

His shoes are ready for red carpet, but bring a sense of occasion to any event. A pair of Manolos will always add a splash of joy to life. Some have said they feel as though they glide through a room when they wear his shoes, that they feel empowered by them; Sarah Jessica Parker claims she could run a marathon in a pair of Manolos, due to the inordinate amount of experience she has hailing cabs and running down avenues in them.

The great and good of fashion adore Blahnik – the late American *Vogue* fashion editor André Leon Talley and *Vogue Italia* editor Franca Sozzani; also Bianca Jagger, Domenico Dolce and Stefano Gabbana, Grace Coddington, David Bailey, Naomi Campbell, Carolina Herrera, Tilda Swinton, Madonna, Sarah Jessica Parker (naturally), Azzedine Alaïa, Joan Rivers, Stephen Jones, and so many more. The great and good of film also wear him: Emma Stone, Uma Thurman, Jessie Buckley, Taika Waititi, Gabrielle Union, Jennifer Lawrence, Emily Blunt, Emma Watson, Elizabeth Debicki…

He has been said to fulfil dreams, create theatre, communicate through shoes, and master perfection and romance. He is at once the Godfather and the Picasso of footwear, and Madonna once claimed his creations are better than sex. His designs have been described as "friends", and gestures, not shoes. He has been dubbed the sultan of slippers, the holy man of heels.

In an interview with Elle.com in 2022, Kristina Blahnik, Manolo's niece – and who took over from Blahnik's sister as company CEO in 2013 – described him not as a shoe designer, but as a creative who just happens to use shoes as his form of expression. They are beautiful objects, she notes, with a timelessness about them.

Memorably, the former editor of British *Vogue*, Alexandra Shulman pointed out that God would not have provided us with Manolo Blahnik if we were destined to wear flat shoes – which clearly we were not. Though, as a side note, Blahnik does do those, too!

# London Fashion Week Debut

One could be forgiven for thinking that Manolo Blahnik would be a stalwart at the industry trade show that is Fashion Week, which takes place twice a year in London – one of fashion's four capitals. His shoes, after all, have been worn by many of its attendees and wandered regularly

LEFT: Michael Roberts and Manolo Blahnik, 2016.

down runways for designers (in 2007 he collaborated with Christopher Kane and Aquascutum).

But it wasn't until 2013 that Blahnik made his London Fashion Week debut. The designer showcased a film created by Michael Roberts, the late fashion journalist, style director and photographer who would also go on to direct the documentary, Manolo: *The Boy Who Made Shoes for Lizards* in 2017. The pair were great friends.

Speaking to the British Vogue website the same year, the designer confessed the reason it had taken him so long to join the fashion calendar was because he was not a fan of crowds. Having been invited to show so many times before, and noting that it was doing very well, he felt the time was right to connect with more people and make an appearance.

Of course, showing a film rather than doing a catwalk presentation was very on-brand for Blahnik since it tapped into his love for films. It felt natural to showcase his spring/summer 2014 collection in such a way.

The five-minute short featured Rupert Everett and was reportedly inspired by music and silent movies from the turn of the 20th century, which again tapped into his interests. Lucy Birley, a British model, photographer and socialite who began as one of Blahnik's clients aged 16, also featured in it.

Funnily enough, the designer had made no promises about returning to the schedule thereafter, though he would continue to collaborate with some of fashion's biggest names in the next few years. He would also find himself working with some of the biggest names in the world, generally. Cue Rihanna.

# Rihanna

Rihanna had found fame for hits including "We Found Love" and "Umbrella". She told American Vogue online that she wanted to work with Manolo because of the craftsmanship for which he was so well known. The news broke in March 2016 to much buzz and instant speculation as to whether there would be more.

The songstress launched her own lingerie and fashion brands, Savage x Fenty and Fenty, in 2018 and 2019 respectively (Fenty Beauty debuted in 2017).

Talking to Glamour.com in 2016, Blahnik shared how the 9-to-5 boot was designed for Rihanna. She had wanted a thigh-high denim boot that linked to the waist via a belt – and he'd done something similar in the past. The result was exactly as it sounds – a long leg in denim all the way up to the thigh, embellished on the inner side with just a flash of flesh. It was a bold design, a little like chaps. Very brave, very Rihanna.

Blahnik had met Rihanna at the British Fashion Awards (now rebranded as the Fashion Awards) in 2012 and during the summer of 2015, she approached him about the collaboration. She had already been wearing his shoes and he liked her music.

Among the rest of the collection, which was rendered

in denim at Rihanna's suggestion, was a cowgirl boot and a strappy sandal, as well as a sequin pointy stiletto pump.

It would not be the end of their creative endeavours together – there would be a further two collections released, which would be just as statement-making.

The 9-to-5 design was included in the Barbican's exhibition "The Vulgar", which ran from October 2016 to February 2017 and celebrated fashion's relationship with so-called bad taste. The exhibition featured a series of films in which Blahnik, plus other contemporary designers, discussed their associations with the word vulgar.

# Menswear

Despite the strong association with soaring heels, Manolo Blahnik began by creating men's footwear in the 1970s. He was making men's shoes before he got his big break with Ossie Clark. According to the Manolo Blahnik biography, written by Colin McDowell, he made a range of saddle shoes which, though not a commercial success, were worn by his friends including Peter Schlesinger and the artist David Hockney.

Menswear shoes would not necessarily be his focus for the years that followed – though the "Manolo" is a men's design he designed and wore himself, especially during the 1980s (and to this day). It was the first menswear design to be translated into a womenswear style, its proportions reduced to suit smaller feet.

In recent years, he has reintroduced men's shoes to his offering, giving men a chance to enjoy the kind of footwear thrills women have long had. Unsurprisingly, colour is key – as is a sense of glamour and sophistication. These are not trend-driven designs, but classic designs that will last. It should be noted that slippers and loafers are especially popular among the fashion set – slippers are the ideal shoe to anchor an eveningwear look.

OPPOSITE: Manolo Blahnik at the brand's Burlington Arcade store launch, 2016.

Blahnik has also had a menswear pop-up in prestigious department store Harrods. In 2018, a dedicated menswear store opened alongside a womenswear store in London's historic Burlington Arcade.

# Accolades

Manolo Blahnik has dressed countless feet and been there for many an important moment in fashion and culture (how many awards have been won in Manolo Blahniks?). He has received many prestigious accolades in recognition of this. They include: an Honorary Doctorate by the Royal Society of Arts and an Honorary Doctorate of Arts by the Royal College of Art in 2001; La Medalla de Oro en Merito en las Bella's Artes by the King of Spain in 2002; an Honorary CBE from Her Majesty Queen Elizabeth II to recognise the fact that he was one of the most successful and influential designers of our time in 2007. The then-Culture Secretary, James Purnell told press: "Manolo Blahnik is one of only a handful of designers whose name is synonymous with their product."

BELOW: Manolo Blahnik at the British
Fashion Awards 2012 at the Savoy Hotel.

# Awards

Blahnik has also been recognised with a host of awards. The British Fashion Council awarded him in 1990, 1999 and 2003. He scooped prizes from *Footwear News* in 1998 and again in 2003; he was presented with the Rodeo Drive Walk of Style award in 2008, and in 2011 received the *Footwear News* Lifetime Achievement Award, presented by Carolina Herrera. That same year he received the Savannah College of Art and Design André Leon Talley award. And in 2012 he was awarded the British Fashion Council Outstanding Achievement Award as well as the prestigious Premio Nacional de Diseño de Moda in Spain.

In 2015, Blahnik was given the Lifetime Achievement award at the *Elle* Style Awards, presented to him by Naomi Campbell.

PREVIOUS: Manolo Blahnik among the winners at the British Fashion Awards 2012.

LEFT: Manolo Blahnik with Naomi Campbell.

# Collaborations, Part 2

As fashion progressed into the 21st century, collaborations became a fundamental part of the business, where before they had been a novelty. The team-ups became bolder and better. And Manolo Blahnik didn't shy away from getting involved – the past decade has seen some standout, if not surprising, pairings for the brand.

## Vetements

Circa 2014, a new brand name entered the fashion universe. Vetements, meaning clothes in French, was launched by Demna Gvasalia and his brother Guram and quickly established itself as the most exciting fashion label around. It was renegade, subversive, championed a sort of distressed normcore, and was the show of Paris Fashion Week to go to – often taking place in sex clubs or far-flung destinations on the outskirts of town.

By 2015, Demna would be the creative director of one of Paris' best-known brands, Balenciaga, but would continue to work on Vetements until 2019, when he officially exited.

In 2016, in a collaborative move to outdo all collaborations so far, Vetements announced it would partner with 18 labels for a collection which was to be shown during couture fashion week in Paris. Among the labels was Manolo

Blahnik. Others
included Juicy
Couture, Comme
des Garçons,
Canada Goose,
Brioni and Reebok
– a real gamut
of brands which
operated across
different spaces in
the industry.

RIGHT: The boots for
Vetements on display.

OVERLEAF LEFT: The
designer collaborated
with Vetements July 2016.

OVERLEAF RIGHT:
Vetements July 2016.

For Blahnik, the team-up included thigh-high-scraping boots – similar to the boots he created with Rihanna, who was spotted on Instagram wearing them – all of which sold out on e-tailer Net-A-Porter when they were released. There were also pointy-toed pumps and slingbacks in jarring bright colours, but it was the boots that stole the show. How could they not, eye-catching as they were?

The idea behind the mega-collaboration was to take an iconic product from each brand and put it through the Vetements lens. Blahnik had developed the "Wader" in the late 1980s, and again for Alaïa around 1992–3. The Vetements boots were included in "The Art of Shoes" exhibition at Palazzo Morando, Milan.

# Birkenstock

It might not be what you expect from someone who specialises in designing and making beautiful and exuberant footwear but according to Blahnik, Birkenstocks – known for their sturdy, reliable and practical design – have always been a part of his wardrobe. He was happy to be able to combine his style with their everyday aesthetic for a collaboration in 2022 – which sold out almost immediately. It had come about as a result of Manolo himself being photographed for a campaign, in which he was captured wearing his Birkenstocks in his own environment.

The limited-edition collection took the Birkenstock Arizona and Boston styles and rendered them in velvet in jewel hues of magenta and blue, as well as black leather. Each was finished off with the designer's signature mirror buckle – lounge luxe indeed. A further drop of the covetable collection saw punchy polka dots added into the mix.

# Wales Bonner

Grace Wales Bonner became a breakout star of British Fashion when she launched her menswear label in 2014, following her graduation from Central Saint Martins. She is known for her fusion of European heritage and Afro Atlantic spirit and has scooped a host of awards during her career so far, including Emerging Menswear Designer at the British Fashion Awards, and collaborated with brands such as Dior, Anderson & Sheppard and Manolo Blahnik.

Bonner and Blahnik teamed up for her autumn/winter 2017 collection. According to *Footwear News*, the pair had a mutual admiration for one another. The collection was inspired by street preachers and Renaissance street characters – the idea was to merge historic references with contemporary ones. She was also interested in African sandals and exotic skins.

Blahnik, she said, was excited by the idea. They ended up developing the footwear first – which Blahnik said took months – and building the ready-to-wear collection around it.

OPPOSITE: Manolo Blahnik with Grace Wales Bonner, 2017.

# Bridal

B lahnik has been known to say that men have told him his shoes have saved marriages. In 2017, the brand embarked upon bridal – in retrospect, it is somewhat surprising that Blahnik hadn't entered bridal already, especially given the SJP-*SATC* proposal scene.

Married in Manolos was a curated collection of classic styles that could be customised for brides and their guests.

Manolo Blahnik re-released the famed Hangisi in 2018 – the 10th anniversary of the *Sex and the City* film that had made it so famous. The A Decade of Love capsule collection was dedicated to New York City and the Manolo Blahnik woman.

Interestingly, Carrie Bradshaw was not the only one to have a memorable marriage moment with the shoe. The American socialite and fashion influencer Olivia Palermo also wore the shoe for her 2014 wedding.

OPPOSITE: Olivia Palermo at the 80th Venice International Film Festival, 2023.

# On Screen, Elvis

Watching films is a favourite pastime of Manolo Blahnik's, and his shoes have featured in many a silver screen moment. In 2022, he worked with the award-winning costume designer Catherine Martin to create custom shoes for Baz Luhrmann's *Elvis* film starring Austin Butler.

It was the second time they had worked together – they also collaborated in 2001 on the Oscar-winning *Moulin Rouge*. Blahnik's other screen moments include: as worn by Lady Gaga in *The House of Gucci*, 2021; Mary-Janes on Margot Robbie in *The Wolf of Wall Street*, 2013; Bella Swan wears them to marry Edward Cullen in *Twilight Breaking Dawn, Part 1*, 2011; *Gossip Girl*, the original series with Blake Lively and Leighton Meester, 2007–2012; Anne Hathaway's makeover in *The Devil Wears Prada*, 2006; Juliet's gladiator sandals to her angel fancy dress costume in Luhrmann's *Romeo + Juliet*, 1996 and Catherine Deneuve's Yves Saint Laurent outfits came with Manolo's Julia pumps in *The Hunger*, 1983.

In *Elvis*, Elvis Presley, played by Austin Butler, and Jerry Schilling, played by Luke Bracey, both wear Manolos inspired by existing Manolo Blahnik shapes: his Tupelo design, which is a black and white lace-up; Victor, a white calf leather boot; and Graceland, a toggle desert boot.

Blahnik finds himself drawn to the 1950s for inspiration, especially when it comes to his menswear designs. He said that working with costume designer Martin on the *Elvis* film was an honour and a privilege.

BELOW: An Elvis billboard: Blahnik designed shoes for Baz Luhrmann's *Elvis* film.

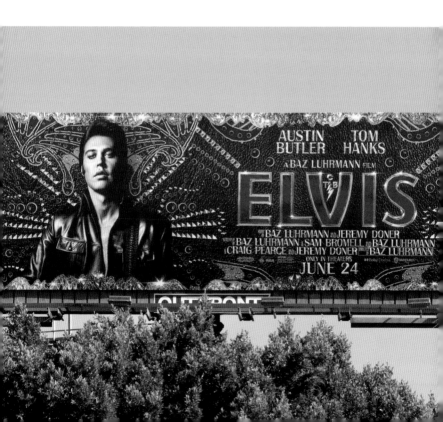

# Manolo Blahnik
# Meets Barbie

In the summer of 2023, there was only one character and one colour on everyone's mind: Barbie and Barbie pink.

Greta Gerwig's *Barbie* saw Margot Robbie take the titular role, with Ryan Gosling as her Ken. Throughout the film's press tour and on the red carpet, Robbie would often dress in outfits that mimicked the wardrobe of her iconic plastic counterpart. Her feet were adorned with heels custom-designed by Manolo Blahnik.

Heels are, of course, a mainstay of the Barbie wardrobe owing to the doll's high-arched foot. When asked to create shoes for the movie, Blahnik turned to some of his most successful designs and gave them a bit of a Barbie update.

Among the styles he used were his BB pumps and Jada mules, which came in pink. He told Vogue.co.uk at the time that pink was among his favourite colours and that he was a fan of both the character and the actress playing her.

It was an ideal match – one icon dressing another.

OPPOSITE: Margot Robbie, dressed the part, at a Barbie press conference, 2023.

# The Craft

The focus of Blahnik's work is the real-life craft, the touch of the hand, Blahnik's own attention to detail and his desire to be at the factories during the process – the real artisanal experience. But the brand has also embraced the digital world in recent years and used it to enhance its craftsmanship focus.

In 2021, the brand debuted The Manolo Blahnik Archives – commemorating 50 years of Manolo Blahnik. It offered fans and customers a better understanding of the brand and its history via an addition to the website.

The Craft was added to this in 2023 – a new space which celebrates the craftsmanship of each shoe and shares insights behind the making, such as sketches, fine details and the journey of the shoe from concept to finished product.

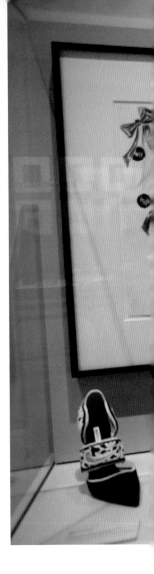

ABOVE: Inside Manolo Blahnik's
*The Art of Shoes* exhibition, 2017.

OVERLEAF: Manolo Blahnik
sketching in his office.

# Standout Shoes

The Hangisi is perhaps the most iconic Manolo style, but there are other equally well-known and much-adored Manolo Blahnik shoes.

The Lurum is another crystal-embellished design which easily satisfies a Hangisi fan's taste. The sheaf-like sparkle spills across the front of the shoe and across the front of the ankle, a little like a mule.

Another *SATC* favourite is the Sedaraby D'Orsay sandal, also with a jewelled buckle. Once Carrie Bradshaw finally receives her replacement pair (recall "A Woman's Right To Shoes"), she jubilantly takes them for a spin around the block.

In 2023, the designer shared with *Vogue* his five favourite shoes from his 50-year career. They included the Antoinetta, the shoe he designed for the Marie Antoinette film. He felt the design was the sort of thing *Marie Antoinette* would have worn today.

The BB pump was another – named, he said, after Brigitte Bardot. It is a classic shoe with wear-with-everything appeal.

The Campari was a shoe he designed in the 1990s, inspired by a picture Corinne Day had taken of Kate Moss. He said he took the classic Mary Jane and essentially made it sexier, with a pointed toe, a high heel and black patent leather. This is the source of Carrie Bradshaw's great excitement in the Vogue closet.

The Maysale was formerly known as Salem as it had been inspired by the collars and cuffs worn by pilgrims as they travelled to America on the Mayflower. It was created for the fashion designer Isaac Mizrahi's spring/summer 1991 collection. A mule with a big buckle on the front, they were also worn by Madonna and Linda Evangelista. Blahnik says he particularly likes the way a mule makes you walk.

And finally, there was the Carolyne which he designed in 1986. It is inspired by the artist Carolyne Roehm and was worn by Carolyn Bessette-Kennedy. Blahnik points out that it is not tied to any particular era and is akin to a universal shoe, ideal for wearing anywhere, any time, any place.

Other shoes Blahnik has name-checked in interviews include the fetishistic Arre

OPPOSITE: Anna Wintour
at London Fashion Week,
spring/summer 2013.

ABOVE: Anna Wintour at
London Fashion Week,
spring/summer 2015.

LEFT: Anna Wintour at the
Burberry show, 2012.

RIGHT: Anna Wintour at the
premiere of *Harry Potter
and The Deathly Hallows
Part 2*, London, 2011.

and the panelled Gurzuf
boot. Of course, there
is also the Callasli,
favoured by Anna
Wintour, and reportedly
made by Blahnik to her
preferred specifications.
The shoes – which the
press notes she has been
wearing since 1994 –
feature two intersecting
straps at the front
and have a slingback.
Originally, they had an
ankle strap.

Wintour has many
pairs, hence Blahnik
nicknaming them "AW",
and they are created
from several special lasts
that fit her foot exactly.
You will clock the style
on the editor's feet
during fashion week and
glamorous events.

Meanwhile, one that can't help but stand out is the recently rebranded Ossie shoe, featuring cherries and leaves, which he designed for Ossie Clark for the spring/summer 1972 collection. But it is not the mishap he encountered that makes it memorable – it is the captivating design, which winds up around the leg. *T Magazine* reported in 2023 that it was inspired by laurel leaves from Alexander the Great. And, according to the *New York Post*, the design reappeared again in 1997.

In 2012, Blahnik created a very sparkly crystal-covered satin bootie for Bergdorf Goodman's 111th anniversary, called the Lacelimi.

Despite a great many wonderful confections, Blahnik has said that, today, the best shoes are the simple ones. He himself is often spotted in an elegant slipper.

ABOVE: Botanical inspired designs.

OPPOSITE: A tassel design for spring/ summer 2014 at London Fashion Week.

# 100 Million Milestone

In October 2023, it was announced that the Manolo Blahnik brand – which has operated as a private company – experienced quite the milestone, with sales exceeding 100m euros: 2022 had been a record financial year at 118.2m euros, up 69 per cent from 69.9m euros in 2021.

The great success was attributed to a thirst for glamour after the pandemic, as well as being helped by sales at its Madison Avenue and East Hampton stores. They had both opened in summer 2021.

There had also been a push in menswear, it was noted. Speaking about the milestone, Kristina Blahnik, the CEO of the company since 2013, reiterated that they were jewellers of shoes. And the good news didn't end there – a move and a new premises were incoming.

OPPOSITE: Manolo Blahnik poses for a photoshoot in London, 2006.

# Old Burlington Street

Following on from Blahnik's Burlington Arcade store, which opened its doors to cocktails and book signings in 2016, the business moved into an elegant Georgian townhouse on Old Burlington Street in 2023. Previously, it had premises at Vigo Street.

A reported £35
million deal
was secured on
number 31 Old
Burlington Street,
a Grade 1 listed
and recently
refurbished
building that was
about to become
the brand's new
HQ. According
to the *Financial
Times*, it was
built by Lord
Burlington in
1718.

Also in 2023, Elodie Bougenault was named global Chief
Commercial Officer, tasked with leading expansion plans,
focussing on Asia. It came after the brand had won a battle
for its IP in the Supreme People's Court of the People's
Republic of China in 2022.

# Manolo, the Man

In any interview with Manolo Blahnik, there is a prevailing theme: he talks a mile a minute with a mind full of thoughts and ideas he can't contain. This is something he will happily discuss with his interviewer, who is usually enthralled – he notes few people can keep up, including his friends. He is as energetic as ever and eager to get on with his work. Though, he confesses that a lot of the time he is quite silent.

He draws at home as well as at work. One place he calls home is Bath, Somerset – he fell for the charms of its 18th-century architecture, residing in a royal crescent property he bought in the 1980s. With its sweeping Regency facades and elegant buildings, it is a city that feels very Manolo.

The designer also still calls the Canaries home, too. When there, he enjoys spending time with his dogs, relaxing and going for walks in the mountains – though he usually still does a spot of work. He told the *Guardian* in 2022 that he couldn't comprehend the idea of retirement.

He loves his dogs and confesses he is addicted to his labradors – he says he prefers creatures to people. To Manolo, bliss is walking in the countryside with his dogs.

PREVIOUS: Manolo Blahnik at the launch of his Burlington Arcade shop.

OPPOSITE: Manolo Blahnik at the British Fashion Awards.

He is a morning reader, which he says is good for the soul – he likes to get lost in the pages of the books he is reading, explaining that they can inspire him in unforeseen ways, and that he loves the descriptions, especially of the fashion.

He is described as being as iconic as his shoes: a striking silhouette adorned with round glasses, bow ties and double-breasted suits – he cuts a dash.

Despite a noted love of history, black-and-white films and motifs from the past that clearly feature among his designs, Blahnik says he doesn't like to dwell on the past too much. The future is greatly appealing to him, partly because he feels his greatest achievements are yet to come. This is an exciting prospect for a man who has already done so much, created so much, dressed so many feet, won so many awards, defined fashions and designed so many fantastic shoes.

Despite all of his success, he still doesn't believe he has perfected his craft, which is a refreshing if not novel approach to have. He still draws and designs every shoe and bag he creates.

Among his most recent designs are pumps and sandals featuring metallic gold hardware, super strappy slingbacks, raffia mules and ballet flats; mules with ruched detailing that have a wisp of historic drama, and dainty bow details. And, of course, updates of the now legendary favourites and classics, for which Manolo, the man and brand, are much loved.

OPPOSITE: Historic Bath, one of the places Manolo Blahnik calls home.

ABOVE: On the set of *Il Gattopardo* (The Leopard), directed by Luchino Visconti, one of Blahnik's favourite films.

RIGHT: The man behind jewellery for the feet, Manolo Blahnik.

# Image Credits

(t) = top, (b) = bottom, (c) = centre, (l) = left, (r) = right

Page 5 Patrick McMullan/Getty; 7 Kristine Larsen/Getty; 8-9 JP Yim/Getty; 11 Rose Hartman/Getty; 12-13 Dave Benett/Getty; 15 Jan Wlodarczyk/Alamy; 16 Wirestock, Inc./Alamy; 18 colaimages/Alamy; 19 Frédéric VIELCANET/Alamy; 20-21 Keystone Press/Alamy; 23 MediaPunch Inc/Alamy; 24-25 ZUMA Press, Inc./Alamy; 26-27 ZUMA Press, Inc./Alamy; 28 Independent/Alamy; 29 Everett Collection Inc/Alamy; 31 Nobby Clark/Popperfoto/Getty; 32 Bentley Archive/Popperfoto/Getty; 34 Evening Standard/Getty; 35 WWD/Getty; 37 Evening Standard/Getty; 39 Jonathan Becker/Getty; 40 Retro AdArchives/Alamy; 42-43 Europa Press Entertainment/Getty; 45 David M. Benett/Getty; 46 Patti McConville/Alamy; 47 NurPhoto/Getty; 48 NurPhoto/Getty; 49 NurPhoto/Getty; 50 Vittorio Zunino Celotto/Getty; 51 Retro AdArchives/Alamy; 52 mikecphoto/Shutterstock; 54 WWD/Getty; 56 Europa Press Entertainment/Getty; 57 NurPhoto/Getty; 58 Ben A. Pruchnie/Getty; 59 Europa Press Entertainment/Getty; 60-61 NurPhoto/Getty; 63 PA Images/Alamy; 65 WWD/Alamy; 66 WWD/Getty; 68 Everett Collection Inc/Alamy; 69 Retro AdArchives/Alamy; 70 Everett Collection Inc/Alamy; 71 (t) NurPhoto/Getty; 71 (b) Europa Press Entertainment/Getty; 73 James Devaney/Getty; 74-75 WWD/Getty; 77 Ron Galella, Ltd/Getty; 78 Bruce Glikas/Getty; 79 Getty Images/Getty; 80-

81 George Napolitano/Getty; 83 John Stoddart/Popperfoto/ Getty; 84-85 PA Images/Alamy; 86-87 Everett Collection Inc/ Alamy; 88 Nathaniel Noir/Alamy; 91 WENN Rights Ltd/Alamy; 92-93 United Archives GmbH/Alamy; 95 Dave Benett/Getty; 96-97 Max Mumbly/Indigo/Getty; 99 Retro AdArchives/ Alamy; 100-101 Paul Greaves/Alamy; 102-103 WWD/Getty; 104 Robin Platzer/Getty; 106 David M. Benett/Getty; 108-109 David M. Benett/Getty; 111 Europa Press Entertainment/Getty; 113 David M. Benett/Getty; 114-115 Ian Gavan/Getty; 116-117 Mike Marsland/Getty; 118-119 David M. Benett/Getty; 121 CTK/ Getty; 122 Estrop/Getty; 123 Estrop/Getty; 125 Estrop/Getty; 127 Dave Benett/Getty; 128-129 Stefania D'Alessandro/Getty; 131 AaronP/Bauer-Griffin/Getty; 133 Han Myung-Gu/Getty; 134-135 Europa Press Entertainment/Getty; 136-137 Ian Cook/ Getty; 139 MEGA/Getty; 140 Nick Harvey/Getty; 141 Doug Peters/Alamy; 142 Mike Marsland/Getty; 143 Allstar Picture Library Ltd/Alamy; 144 Anrephoto/Shutterstock; 145 Ben A. Pruchnie/Getty; 146-147 Lorenzo Agius/Getty; 148 David M. Benett/Getty; 149 David M. Benett/Getty; 150-151 Ian Gavan/ Getty; 153 Rune Hellestad- Corbis/Getty; 154 Matt Cardy/ Getty; 155 ullstein bild Dtl./Getty; 156-157 CTK/Alamy

OVERLEAF: The designer
is a fan of dogs, here at
a book party.

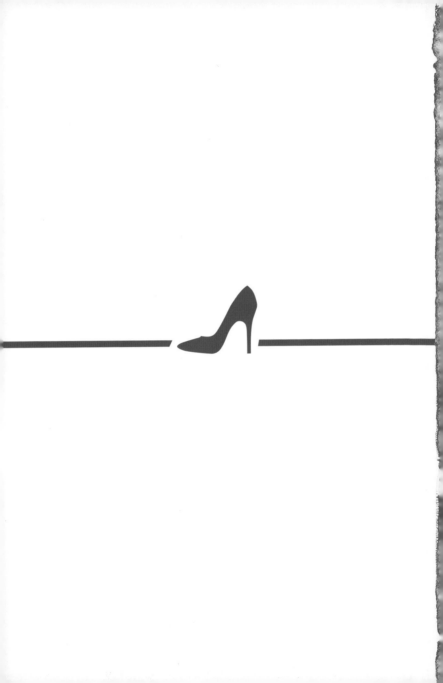